www.finishinglinepress.com

Natural Wonders

poems by

Sarah Sutro

Finishing Line Press
Georgetown, Kentucky

Natural Wonders

ACKNOWLEDGMENTS

Thanks to the Duxbury Writer's Retreat for time to work and great friendship
with other writers

Publisher: Leah Huete de Maines
Editor: Christen Kincaid
Cover Art: Sarah Sutro
Author Photo: Laura Blacklow, http://www.laurablacklow.com
Cover Design: Elizabeth Maines McCleavy

Order online: www.finishinglinepress.com
              also available on amazon.com

Author inquiries and mail orders:
Finishing Line Press
PO Box 1626
Georgetown, Kentucky 40324
USA

Contents

for Will, Beth and Hazel

Present Tense

on the screened-in porch
on Chincoteague Island
sea oats and pampas
grass
move across
my vision in waves—
the way colored
beams of light
waver
against steam
below the waterfall,
at home

a black vulture
hunches over
the top of a dead
tree,
while
on the
Northern
River
a bird
balances
on a floating branch,
its head turned
away

pinkish
masses of oat
seeds tinged
with dawn's
sharp light
illumine grasses,
blade by blade

A Still Morning

eleven fat geese
bathe in the river's
shallow water

black and white moths
rise
from the grass

a quiet August morning,
the river less
tempestuous,
almost a sleeping god,
one that supports wild birds
and beasts that come
to drink

a monarch rests on
a tomato plant,
closing and opening
its wings:

a summer day
in the Berkshires

Light: Things Seen

shadow of leaf
and leaf
itself—
which is illusion?
which real?
light around
objects
defines them,
and shadow
sharpens the edges
of what we see

light
plays over
things,
without
possession:
becomes the object
of what is seen

how often I
watch the center,
instead of the
periphery—
where all things
happen:

center
of my life,
whom
I have no power
to keep or stay—
light gathers
around your face,
an early winter halo,
like snow.

age well,
explore the world with me
watch the light

Shadows

deer pass through
the trees like
shadows
rain falls
gently on
moss,
rocks,
woods.
pausing
here,
thoughts of
where we are
in time,
the present,
our own
company.

light falls
slant
and then
rain falls
again

Natural Anarchy

against white water
a white moth
follows me to the top
of the dam,
moving here, there,
disappearing
against the foam
now a spiraling black one rises
up from the grass

under the river
bands of silt
blend as the water flows.
froth moves in flocks across the surface,
like birds
but where are the birds now,
the ones I saw earlier this summer?

staring at the flowers
on my table—
beyond restrictions—
everything has changed:
a new world.
yet I am thrilled
to be in this life, alive

a sandpaper chorus of
late summer crickets,
shadows spread under
the maple tree
in a deep viridian pool
Queen Anne's lace dotting
yards where no one has mowed,
dark centers a pause
in all this anarchy

Explanation

If night is a pearl,
  where is the oyster?
If the moon is a worn
  shoe, who is wearing it?
If the trees against a
  violet sky are scratchy
  fingers,
Where is the handwriting,
  on the sky?

The edges of buildings,
  frosted white, are a
  geometric painting.
Black crows crossing
  the dawn are stitches
  in a vast quilt.
The ribbon of highway
  outside my window
  is a torrent
  of horses

Perimeter

of yellow leaves
beneath a green tree,
lush red berries
of fall:
dark purple pods,
red sumac—
accumulate,
expand
crescendo

unzipping
her leather coat,
approaching
the building,
a meeting
up the worn stairs,
plants on the landing,
teal steps,
pale yellow walls—

and the world
beyond—
explodes,
not in leaves,
nor sumac:
but in tempests,
war, yet
the small union
of where they live,
continues

Wherever you are

in Oakland
by the window
of the Mexican restaurant
when riot police, shields upheld, suddenly
charge—
the center in chaos

or the coup in Bangkok,
quiet reigning
on the city,
empty streets as a
line of tanks
pass

and mobs
near the house in Dhaka
protesting US bombing
of Afghanistan,
burned buses by the side of the road,
university shootings,
life as usual

here, now—
two days since storming
the Capitol:
filters down to each of us
wherever we are—
guns, flags, t-shirts urging
violence

yet wherever you are,
whoever you are:
   the beauty
   of the woods
   remains

Territory

where is the wood
where the owl once
lived?
where he flew straight
at me, thinking
an animal,
perhaps,
another owl

dense growth
by the side of
the road where I
walk
now trees cut
and a clear view—
to where?
a house,
a yard.

these small remnants
of wildness
are all
there are
for owls,
and walkers
like me

late Summer

the Rose of Sharon
insinuates itself
among the decks
which tells me fall
is next

though no one's saying
August's up we know
summer's past
its fullest show

while basil blooms
and red
tomatoes
ripen,
light declines
and we spend time inside,
instead

red
tomatoes ripen,
light
declines and
we spend time
inside,
instead

I heard thunder

wild thyme
grows on the upper banks
and the blue heron
rises up from
the rocks
white water eddies
down the river
in patterns—
a hot summer
afternoon.

The world unfurls
around the image
of a black man in pain,
a pattern
that repeats
and
repeats

at 4am
I couldn't sleep
reading about
slave states
then it began
to rain
first soft,
gentle, then slick
heavy downpour
still awake,
drinking amaretto
early morning, as if night.
now really raining,
few cars streak past
I hear thunder

Mid-Afternoon

a perfect balance
of blue and purple:
light spilling across
the floor,
a moment
which time stands
uncounted—
only the whir of the
overhead fan,
a book beside me
on the table

on the ferry
coming closer
to land
dolphins two by two
arch
into waves,
surround the boat
like protection,
communing,
or coming home

when we arrived
a cardinal and a myrtle cluster
two reds on the same branch
orange-red and dark rose,
nature expresses
two things
simultaneously

in perfect balance

Neon Leaf

Glowing
rim of red
around a leaf—
the rubber tree lit
by light from the window,
a thin electric line of fire—why
on a day when I do everything
backwards: not thinking, not
approaching
things
the same
ordinary way

A solid rubber tree suddenly seems not solid,
three dimensional, then not—
What makes light leap
around things,
illumine the reality
of what is there?

to start again

autumn flowers gone,
brusque winter winds
bring with them
doubt, end of year thoughts—
and maybe skiing through a wood

waiting for news and
hoping for better times—
no capitol incursion,
no gun violence,
no virus.
but maybe a light snow—
pushing off into a field on skis

if only
this was everything,
a cure, like clearing the
desk, clearing
the mind,
a way to say
enough,
to start again,

give thanks
again

On Thanksgiving Day

light falls
gently
  on the far hill,
picks up
edges
of leaves,
pale orange

it's quiet on the road—
sumac candles glow
softly red
by the creek

scattered across
the dark mountain
yellow trees—
a few flame
fuchsia

and yesterday: golden leaves,
red berries
tumbled with
sunlight—
white hawk
rose above me as I
walked down the
leafed lane;
cones of fire
rose on my left,
by the river

all is time
connected,
as if by a thread—
and down the way
the blue door waits

Deep Blue

deep blue rises
in the sky like
irises
in the early, dark mornings
of December
uneven
line
of trees
appear across the window,
sounds of traffic
steer across the road,
holidays pass
like ghosts—
how to connect the celebration
with dark tones of our time?
yet the blue gets brighter, blooms….
while roses on the table glow rich
in their redness,
and the coffee smells good

now lights
reflect in the
window, a
lighted tree
where there is
none.
scumbling, tumbling, soft forms of buildings
across the road and tree trunks appear,
like a world rehearsing the next scene—

actors on this set, we wait for our lines and cues,
to begin the play, ready with costume, character,
color
in this darkened time

Snow above, snow below

River snowed-over,
wet trees leaning
toward the dam—
massive ice clusters
cling
to concrete—
frozen spray—
only dark
patches of water
beneath

while down the way
a blue door beckons
in the cold,
through ice
and cold wind:

like moss through snow
green bleeding through,
water coming fast,
rising

Provincetown

crossing the bridge
into another world
the sea
beyond the crest
as
maple leaves
rust and yellow,
drift from
trees

pearl, oyster,
sky changes
reflect
evanescent paintings
air settling
over borders,
dissolves
the landscape

gazing at the
back hill
through
fog

nacreous,
swirls

the day passes

Yet Night Comes on with Beauty

bombs crash a world away
and people flee—
night covers,
a quilt of stars
that neither explain nor mourn
night being like this—
the blue violet hours
when all is tinged with beauty

forests
have been ruined before
and come back....
let one leaf fall
to show me the cycles are
still working
let me hear water
in the channel, running
and birds that
linger above the dam,
merganser and the mallard
come back—

give me morning when
the sun cracks open like
an egg, light spilling
out like a yolk,
the innocence
of climbing the grassy hill in
new sneakers made
of canvas, and
squish of grass
underfoot.

what the flowers are saying is:
go to the center
with marks leading down petals.
I get the message
as if I were a bee,
heading for a flower.
the ebullient
white flowers,
pink markings leading
into the core.

I surprised a blue heron
who flew up the river today—
this is exactly where I
want to be:
walking a path through
a field by the river;
mild heat,
birds around,
feeling the shade of trees
and the movement of the
water

a lesson in life,
an urging towards
beauty and the deeper
message

End of Year Thoughts

and end of world worries—
the sun composes us
as usual—
while fossils in their ancient beds
lie mute for
millions of years
in a moment ice mountains
    calve into sea
yet being the trees on the hill,
ripe oranges in the blue
    green-swirled bowl,
wind moving across
mountain in winter,
heat
touching ferns'
leaves in summer
we touch
both:
vast time
and identity with all things.
this, that,
wind, trees
…..eating lunch
on the old
pine table—

being kind to the world
is being kind
to ourselves
awareness stretched
as far as
the horizon.

Originally from the Boston area, **Sarah Sutro** studied writing at Tufts University Women's School and BCAE, and art at Cornell, Yale at Norfolk, and the University of the Arts, London.

She has taught writing in the interdisciplinary programs IRO— Lesley University and Union Institute and University; and art at Emerson College, Mass College of Art and Design, SMFA, Pine Manor College, UMass Boston, Cornell, Ithaca College, Boston State College and Lesley College of Art & Design (MFA program).

She is the author of the poetry book *Études* (Finishing Line Press) and a book of essays, *COLORS: Passages through Art, Asia and Nature* (Blue Asia Press). Her poetry has been published internationally, including *International Poetry Review; Amsterdam Quarterly; Panoply, Journal of the Intelligent Traveler; Rockhurst Review; The Big Chili* (BKK); *Die Brucke #9;* and *The Hard Work of Hope* (Mass Poetry).

Anthologies including her work are *Improv (Simplicity in the 21st Century); Bangkok Blondes; Boston, Bangkok, Brattleboro: Alien Pens on Familiar Places; Unbearable Uncertainty; Life Stories; From the Finger Lakes; the Ithaca Women's Anthology,* and *Anthology of Universal Oneness (India).*

She was a finalist both for the Robert Frost Poetry Award and the Mass Cultural Council Poetry grant. She has had residencies at MacDowell Colony, Millay Colony, Ossabaw Island Foundation, Blue Mountain Center, Art Dulcinium-Montenegro, and the American Academy in Rome.

After several years living in Thailand and Bangladesh, she has settled in the Northern Berkshires, MA. Her art work can be seen at *www.sarahsutro.com.*